Power Words For The Sales Professional

The ULTIMATE Guide
To
Power Words & Marketing Phrases

Justin Hammonds

Inspire Publications

A Division of

Inspire Consultants

For information about special discounts for bulk purchases, please contact: sales@inspireconsultants.com

Inspire Consultants can bring this author to your live event. For more information or to book an event contact: speakers@inspireconsultants.com

ISBN-10:0615550908

ISBN-13:978-0615550909

Dedication

This book is dedicated to the Sales Professionals who have given me the opportunity to help develop them. It's a privilege. Thank you.

Acknowledgements

To my wife and children: Three power words for you.
I Love You

Thank you to my coaches Zig Ziglar, Brendon Burchard, Brian Tracy, and John Maxwell for all the advice and wisdom they have shared over the years. The powerful words you use have shaped my career.

To my Lord and Savior, Jesus Christ: Your words have changed my life and the world forever. I thank you for your grace and mercy. To you may the glory be.
Matthew 10:32

Table of Contents

Introduction

Words, regardless if they are spoken or written, have the ability to create powerful emotions and thoughts. They can encourage and inspire people to perform at incredible levels. For the sales professional words can be the difference of barely getting by or earning a great living. I trust you are more interested in earning a great living and that is why you are taking action to learn these powerful words and phrases. Compiled within these pages are thousands of proven power words and phrases that you will be able to use to get the desired response.

At my workshops I'm often asked about power words, my advice is always the same, I start by asking them, What makes a word a "power word"? This confuses most, but it's not meant to be a trick. The answer is, how you use the word. Power words are words that produce emotions. Ultimately we want those emotions to translate into action. However, practically any word can become a power word if used correctly and with purpose.

It is important to know the purpose of every communication that you have. Unfortunately most sales people never really think about the purpose of their communication. They believe the purpose is to sell and that is incorrect. If you approach your career with that mind set you will have a very short career. The purpose is to solve problems and create emotion. By problems, I mean their needs, wants, desires, and of course their actual problems. Selling is the result, not the purpose.

Most people view presenting as being in person and delivering a sales message. Actually, it is any form of sales communication such as…

- In Person
- Sales Pages
- Sales Letters
- Copy Writing
- Emails

When you view all your communication as a presentation requiring a clear purpose, you start to choose your words more carefully and can start to leverage their power. Here is my simple 6 Step System for better communication in your presentations.

What Is Your Message?

What is the message you want to get across to your client? It needs to be clear. Cut out language that detracts from the message.

What Do You Want Them To Do?
This should be very clear to both them and you.

What Is Holding Them Back?
What would hold back the average person in your target market?

Address It:
Assure them that their fears are natural but unwarranted.

Give Them The Vision:
Let them know how different their situation will be after you have solved their wants, needs, desires, and problems.

Tell Them What You Want Them To Do:
Tell them the next step; tell them how they can take advantage of your solutions.

Craft your presentation with these thoughts in mind selecting words and making them powerful. Words by them self are powerless, but combined with clarity and purpose, delivered with integrity, they become powerful enough to change the world.

A

Abated

Abbreviated

Abolished

Abridged

Absolute

Absolutely

Absolved

Absorbed

Abstract

Accelerate

Accelerated

Accept

Acclaimed

Accommodate

Accompanied

Accomplish

Accomplished

Accumulate

Accurately

Power Words

Achieve

Achieved

Acknowledgment

Acquire

Acquired

Act

Acted

Action

Activate

Activated

Actuated

Adapt

Adapted

Add

Added

Address

Addressed

Adhered

Adjust

Adjustable

Adjusted

Administer

Administered

Admire

Admired

Admitted

Adopted

Adore

Adrenaline

Advance

Advanced

Advantage

Advertise

Advertised

Advice

Advise

Advised

Advocate

Advocated

Affected

Afford

Affordable

Agree

Agreement

Aid

Aide

Aided

Aired

Alert

Align

All

Allocate

Power Words

Allocated

All-Purpose

Allure

Alluring

Altered

Amazing

Ambitious

Amend

Amended

Amplified

Analysis

Analyze

Analyzed

Announcement

Announcing

Answer

Answered

Anticipate

Anticipated

Anyone

Anytime

Anywhere

Appeal

Appealing

Applied

Apply

Power Words For The Sales Professional

Appoint

Appointed

Appraise

Appraised

Approached

Appropriate

Approval by

Approve

Arbitrate

Arbitrated

Arrange

Arranged

Articulate

Articulated

Ascertain

Ascertained

Asked

Assemble

Assembled

Assess

Assessed

Assign

Assigned

Assist

Assisted

Assume

Power Words

Assumed
Astonish
Astonishing
Astonishment
Astounded
Astounding
Astronomical
Attain
Attained
Attend
Attention
Attract
Attracted
Attractive
Audit
Audited
Augment
Augmented
Authentic
Author
Authored
Authorize
Authorized
Autograph
Autographed
Automate

Automated

Automatic

Automatically

Available

Avalanche

Avert

Avoid

Award

Awarded

Awe

Awesome

B

Balance

Balanced

Bandwagon

Bargain

Basic

Beat

Beautiful

Beauty

Began

Begin

Power Words

Believe
Benchmarked
Beneficial
Benefit
Benefited
Benefits
Best
Better
Beware
Beyond
Bid
Big
Blast
Blockbuster
Blocked
Bolster
Bolstered
Bonanza
Bonus
Bonuses
Booming
Boost
Boosted
Borrowed
Bought
Branded

Breakthrough
Breathtaking
Bridged
Brief
Bright
Brilliant
Broaden
Broadened
Brought
Budget
Budgeted
Build
Built
Buy

C

Calculate
Calculated
Calibrate
Call
Can
Canvass
Canvassed

Power Words

Capture
Captured
Care
Cared
Caring
Cash
Cast
Catalog
Cataloged
Catalogue
Catalogued
Categorize
Categorized
Cater
Cause
Caution
Caution
Centralize
Centralized
Certified
Certified
Chair
Chaired
Challenge
Challenged
Challenging

Power Words For The Sales Professional

Change

Changed

Changes

Channeled

Charge

Charged

Charity

Chart

Charted

Cheap

Check

Checked

Choice

Cinch

Circulated

Clarified

Clarify

Classic

Classified

Classify

Clear

Clearance

Cleared

Clever

Closed

Coach

Power Words

Coached
Co-Authored
Code
Collaborate
Collaborated
Collate
Collect
Collectable
Collected
Colorful
Colossal
Combine
Combined
Comfort
Comfortable
Commence
Commercial
Commission
Commissioned
Commit
Committed
Common
Common-Sense
Communicate
Communicated
Compact

Power Words For The Sales Professional

Comparable

Compare

Compared

Compatibility

Compatible

Compelled

Compelling

Competitive

Compile

Compiled

Complete

Completed

Completely

Complied

Complimentary

Compose

Composed

Compounded

Comprehensive

Compromise

Compute

Computed

Computerized

Conceive

Conceived

Concept

Power Words

Conceptualize
Conceptualized
Concerned
Conciliate
Conclude
Condense
Condensed
Conduct
Conducted
Confer
Confident
Confidential
Confirm
Congrats
Congratulations
Connect
Conserve
Conserved
Consider
Consistent
Consolidate
Consolidated
Construct
Constructed
Consult
Consulted

Power Words For The Sales Professional

Contact

Contribute

Contributed

Control

Controlled

Convenient

Convert

Converted

Convertible

Convey

Conveyed

Convince

Convinced

Cooperate

Coordinate

Coordinated

Copy

Core

Correct

Corrected

Correlate

Correspond

Counsel

Counseled

Coupon

Courage

Crammed

Crazy

Create

Created

Critical

Critique

Critiqued

Crucial

Cultivate

Cultivated

Current

Custom

Customizable

Customize

Customized

Cut

D

Danger

Daring

Dazzling

Dealt

Debate

Debated

Debt-Free

Debug

Debugged

Decentralized

Decide

Decrease

Decreased

Dedicate

Dedicated

Deduce

Deductible

Defend

Defer

Deferred

Define

Definite

Delegate

Delighted

Deliver

Delivered

Demonstrate

Demonstrated

Dependable

Depict

Derive

Describe

Power Words

Described
Description
Deserve
Design
Designated
Designed
Desire
Destiny
Detail
Detailed
Detect
Detected
Determine
Determined
Develop
Developed
Devise
Devised
Devote
Diagnose
Diagnosed
Diagram
Difference
Different
Differentiate
Difficult

Difficulty

Digital

Direct

Directed

Directly

Discharge

Disclose

Discount

Discover

Discovered

Discovery

Discriminate

Discuss

Dispatch

Dispatched

Display

Dissect

Dissembled

Disseminate

Distinguish

Distinguished

Distribute

Distributed

Diversified

Diversify

Divested

Document
Dollars
Dominant
Don't
Donate
Doubled
Download
Draft
Dramatic
Draw
Drew
Drive
Drove
Durability
Durable
Dynamic
Dynamics

E

Eager
Eagerly
Earn
Earned
Ease

Power Words For The Sales Professional

Eased

Easily

Easy

Economical

Edge

Edit

Educate

Educated

Effect

Effected

Effective

Effectively

Efficient

Efficiently

Effortless

Effortlessly

Elastic

Elect

Elegant

Elicit

Elicited

Eligible

Eliminate

Eliminated

Emerging

Emphasize

Power Words

Emphasized
Employ
Enable
Enabled
Enchanted
Encourage
Encouraged
Endeavor
Endorse
Endorsed
Endurance
Enduring
Energetic
Energy
Enforce
Enforced
Engaged
Engineer
Engineered
Enhance
Enhanced
Enhancing
Enjoy
Enjoyment
Enlarge
Enlarged

Power Words For The Sales Professional

Enlighten

Enlist

Enlisted

Enormous

Enrich

Enriched

Ensure

Ensured

Enter

Enterprise

Enterprising

Entertain

Entire

Enumerate

Envied

Envied

Envision

Equal

Equals

Equip

Equipped

Escalated

Essential

Establish

Established

Estimate

Power Words

Estimated
Ethical
Ethical
Evaluate
Evaluated
Exact
Examine
Examined
Exceed
Exceeded
Excellent
Except
Exceptional
Exchange
Exchanged
Excite
Excited
Excitement
Exciting
Exclusive
Execute
Executed
Exempted
Exercise
Exhibit
Exhilarated

Power Words For The Sales Professional

Expand

Expanded

Expansive

Expectation

Expectations

Expedite

Expedited

Expensive

Experience

Experienced

Experiment

Expert

Experts

Explain

Explained

Explode

Exploding

Exploit

Explore

Explored

Explosion

Explosive

Exposed

Express

Extend

Extended

Extension
Extensive
Extra
Extract
Extracted
Extraordinary
Extrapolate
Extreme

F

Fabricate
Fabricated
Fabulous
Facilitate
Facilitated
Fact
Facts
Faithful
Faithfulness
Familiarize
Famous
Fantastic
Fantasy
Fascinate

Power Words For The Sales Professional

Fascinating

Fashion

Fashioned

Fast

Faster

Favorable

Features

Fielded

File

Filter

Final

Finalize

Financed

Financial

Find

Finest

Fix

Flash

Flatter

Flattering

Flexibility

Flexible

Focus

Focused

Foolproof

Forecast

Power Words

Forecasted
Forever
Formalized
Formatted
Formed
Formidable
Formula
Formulate
Fortified
Fortify
Fortunate
Fortunately
Fortune
Forward
Foster
Found
Founded
Frame
Free
Freebie
Freedom
Fresh
Fulfilled
Full
Fully
Fun

Fund

Fundamental

Fundamentals

Funny

Furnish

Furnished

Further

Furthered

Future

G

Gain

Gained

Gaining

Gather

Gathered

Gauge

Gauged

Generate

Generated

Generic

Genius

Genuine

Genuinely

Power Words

Get

Giant

Gift

Gifted

Gifts

Gigantic

Give

Global

Gold

Golden

Good

Gorgeous

Govern

Governed

Graceful

Grade

Graded

Grant

Granted

Grateful

Gratification

Great

Greatest

Greet

Greeted

Grouped

Growth

Guarantee

Guaranteed

Guide

Guided

H

Handle

Handled

Handsome

Handy

Happier

Happily

Happiness

Happy

Hard

Harnessed

Head

Healing

Health

Healthy

Heart

Hearty

Heavy

Power Words

Hefty
Heighten
Help
Helped
Helpful
Helping
High
Highest
Highlight
Highlighted
Hire
Hired
Historic
Honor
Honorable
Hope
Host
Hosted
Hot
Hottest
How
How-To
Huge
Hungry
Hurry

I

Idea
Identified
Identify
Illuminated
Illustrate
Illustrated
Imagination
Imaginative
Imagine
Immediately
Impact
Impacted
Impart
Implement
Implemented
Import
Important
Imported
Imprinted
Improve
Improved
Improvement

Power Words

Improvise
Improvised
Inaugurated
Incentive
Incentives
Incorporate
Incorporated
Increase
Incurred
Independent
Index
Individualize
Indoctrinated
Induced
Inexpensive
Influence
Influenced
Inform
Information
Informative
Initiate
Initiated
Innovate
Innovated
Innovation
Innovative

Power Words For The Sales Professional

Inquired

Insane

Insatiable

Insider

Insight

Insightful

Inspect

Inspected

Inspire

Inspired

Inspiring

Install

Installed

Instant

Instantly

Instigated

Instilled

Institute

Instituted

Instruct

Instructed

Instructive

Insure

Insured

Intangible

Integrate

Power Words

Integrated
Intelligent
Interact
Interacted
Interactive
Interesting
Interface
Interpret
Interpreted
Intervene
Intervened
Interview
Interviewed
Intrigue
Intriguing
Introduce
Introducing
Invent
Invented
Inventoried
Inventory
Invest
Invested
Investigate
Investigated
Investigation

Investment

Invited

Involve

Involved

Isolated

Issued

J

Jesting

Join

Joined

Joy

Judge

Judged

Judgment

Just

Justice

Justified

Justify

K

Keep

Kept
Killer
King
Know
Knowledge

L

Label
Large
Largest
Last
Lasting
Latest
Launch
Launched
Launching
Lavish
Lavishly
Lead
Leader
Leadership
Leading

Power Words For The Sales Professional

Learn

Lecture

Lectured

Led

Legal

Legendary

Legitimate

Leverage

Liability

Liberal

Liberated

License

Lifeblood

Lifetime

Lighten

Lightened

Lightened

Limited

Liquidate

Liquidated

List

Listen

Litigate

Litigated

Live

Lively

Lobbied

Lobby

Localize

Localized

Locate

Located

Log

Logged

Longevity

Love

Loved

Loved by

Low

Lowest

Loyalty

Luxury

M

Magic

Magical

Magnetizing

Mainstream

Maintain

Maintained

Power Words For The Sales Professional

Mammoth

Manage

Managed

Mania

Manufacture

Map

Mapped

Market

Marketed

Marvelous

Massive

Master

Mastermind

Masterminds

Masterpiece

Maximize

Maximized

Maximum

Measure

Measured

Mechanize

Mediate

Mediated

Mega

Memorable

Mentored

Power Words

Merchandised
Merged
Millions
Minimized
Miracle
Model
Modeled
Moderate
Moderated
Modern
Modernize
Modernized
Modified
Modify
Money
Monitor
Monitored
Monumental
More
Most
Motivate
Motivated
Moved
Multiplied

N

Named

Narrate

Narrated

National

Nationwide

Natural

Navigate

Navigated

Neat

Necessary

Need

Negotiate

Negotiated

Netted

Never

New

Newest

Nostalgic

Noted

Noticed

Notify

Nourished

Novel

Now
Nurse
Nursed
Nurture

O

Obligation
Observe
Obsession
Obtain
Obtained
Odd
Offer
Offered
Official
Officiate
Offset
Opened
Operate
Operated
Opportunities
Opportunity
Optional
Orchestrate

Power Words For The Sales Professional

Orchestrated

Order

Ordered

Ordered

Organize

Organized

Orient

Orientate

Oriented

Original

Originate

Originated

Outline

Outstanding

Overcome

Overcoming

Overhaul

Overhauled

Overrated

Oversaw

Oversee

Overwhelming

Ownership

P

Package

Participate

Participated

Patented

Patterned

Perceive

Perfect

Perfection

Perform

Performance

Performed

Perks

Permanent

Perpetual

Personal

Personalized

Perspective

Persuade

Persuaded

Phased

Phenomenal

Photograph

Photographed

Power Words For The Sales Professional

Pilot

Pinpointed

Pioneer

Pioneered

Pioneering

Placed

Plan

Planned

Plus

Polled

Popular

Portable

Portfolio

Position

Positioning

Possibilities

Potent

Potential

Power

Powerful

Practice

Precious

Precise

Precision

Predict

Prefer

Power Words

Preference
Preferred
Premier
Premium
Pre-Paid
Prepare
Prepared
Pre-Qualified
Present
Presented
Preserve
Preserved
Preside
Presided
Prevent
Prevented
Preventive
Preview
Priceless
Pride
Prime
Principal
Principle
Print
Prioritize
Priority

Power Words For The Sales Professional

Private

Privilege

Privileged

Probe

Process

Processed

Procured

Produce

Product

Productivity

Professional

Profiled

Profit

Profitable

Profusely

Program

Programmed

Project

Projected

Promise

Promising

Promote

Promoted

Promotional

Prompt

Prompted

Promptness
Propose
Proposed
Prospected
Prosper
Prosperity
Proved
Proven
Provide
Provided
Provocative
Publicize
Publicized
Publish
Published
Purchase
Purchased
Pursued

Q

Qualified
Qualify
Quality
Quantified

Quantify

Quick

Quickest

Quickly

Quieter

Quoted

R

Raise

Raised

Ran

Rank

Ranked

Rare

Rate

Rated

Raw

Read

Ready

Real

Reason

Recall

Received

Recognize

Power Words

Recommend

Recommended

Reconcile

Reconciled

Record

Recorded

Recovered

Recreate

Recruit

Recruited

Rectified

Rectify

Recyclable

Redesigned

Reduce

Reduced

Refer

Refinance

Refine

Refined

Refundable

Regained

Register

Registered

Regulate

Regulated

Power Words For The Sales Professional

Rehabilitate

Rehabilitated

Reinforce

Reinforced

Reinstated

Rejected

Relate

Related

Release

Reliable

Relief

Remarkable

Remedied

Remodel

Remodeled

Render

Renegotiated

Renew

Reorganize

Repair

Repaired

Replace

Replaced

Report

Reported

Represent

Power Words

Represented

Request

Requested

Research

Researched

Reserve

Resolve

Resolved

Respected

Respond

Responded

Response

Restore

Restored

Restrict

Restructured

Resulted

Results

Retain

Retained

Retire

Retrieve

Retrieved

Returnable

Revamp

Revamped

Power Words For The Sales Professional

Reveal

Revealed

Revealing

Reveals

Revelation

Reversed

Review

Reviewed

Reviewing

Revise

Revised

Revisited

Revitalize

Revitalized

Revolutionary

Reward

Rewarded

Rewards

Rich

Richest

Richly

Riveting

Roaring

Rocketed

Route

Royalties

S

Safe

Safeguarded

Safely

Safer

Sale

Salvaged

Sample

Sampler

Satisfy

Save

Saved

Savings

Savvy

Say

Scan

Scarce

Schedule

Score

Screen

Screened

Script

Scrutinize

Power Words For The Sales Professional

Search

Secret

Secrets

Secure

Secured

Security

Seductive

Segment

Segmented

Seize

Select

Selected

Sensational

Separated

Serious

Serve

Served

Service

Serviced

Settle

Settled

Sex

Sexy

Shape

Shaped

Share

Power Words

Sharp
Sharply
Shocked
Shocker
Shocking
Shortened
Show
Showcase
Showcased
Shrank
Shrewd
Signed
Significant
Simple
Simplified
Simplify
Simplistic
Simply
Simulate
Simulated
Sincere
Sincerely
Sizable
Sizzle
Sizzling
Sketch

Power Words For The Sales Professional

Skill

Skilled

Skyrocket

Slash

Smart

Smash

Soar

Softer

Sold

Solicit

Solicited

Solution

Solve

Solved

Sort

Speak

Spearhead

Spearheaded

Special

Specialize

Specialized

Specified

Specify

Speculated

Speedy

Spill

Power Words

Spoke
Spotlight
Spread
Stabilized
Stable
Staffed
Stage
Staged
Standard
Standardize
Star
Stardom
Start
Startle
Startling
Steered
Stimulate
Stimulated
Stimulating
Stop
Storm
Straighten
Strange
Strategize
Strategized
Streamline

Power Words For The Sales Professional

Streamlined

Strengthen

Strengthened

Stressed

Strong

Structure

Structured

Studied

Study

Stunning

Sturdy

Submit

Submitted

Substantial

Substantiate

Substantiated

Substitute

Substituted

Succeed

Success

Successful

Successfully

Suddenly

Sufficient

Suggest

Suggested

Power Words

Suitable
Summarize
Super
Superior
Superseded
Supervise
Supervised
Supplied
Supply
Support
Supported
Supportive
Supreme
Surging
Surpass
Surpassed
Surprise
Survey
Surveyed
Survival
Sustain
Swarm
Symbolize
Synchronized
Synthesize
Systematize

T

Tabulate

Tabulated

Tail

Tailored

Target

Targeted

Taught

Teach

Technical

Technique

Technology

Tell

Tempting

Tend

Terminate

Terrific

Test

Tested

Theorize

Thinner

Thousands

Power Words

Tightened
Time
Timely
Tip
Today
Took
Top
Total
Tough
Tour
Trace
Traced
Track
Trade
Traded
Traditional
Train
Trained
Transacted
Transcribe
Transfer
Transferred
Transform
Transformed
Translate
Translated

Transmit

Transmitted

Transport

Transported

Transpose

Travel

Treat

Treated

Tremendous

Triple

Tripled

Troubleshot

Truly

Trusting

Truth

Truthful

Try

Tutor

Tutored

Tutored

U

Ultimate

Ultra

Power Words

Unbeatable
Uncover
Uncovered
Undeniably
Under
Underlined
Underpriced
Underrated
Underscore
Underscored
Understand
Understanding
Undertook
Underwrote
Unearthed
Unified
Unique
United
Universal
Universe
Unleash
Unleashed
Unlimited
Unlock
Unparalleled
Unreal

Unsurpassed

Untapped

Untold

Unusual

Updated

Upgraded

Uplifting

Urged

Urgent

Used

Useful

Utilize

Utilized

V

Validated

Valuable

Value

Valued

Variety

Verbalized

Verified

Versatility

Vibrant

Viewed

VIP

Vision

Visit

Visited

Visualize

Visualized

Vital

Vivid

Voiced

Volunteered

Vow

W

Want

Want

Wanted

Warning

Wealth

Wealthy

Weathered

Weigh

Weighed

Weird

Power Words For The Sales Professional

Welcomed

Wholesale

Widen

Widened

Willpower

Win

Winning

Wisdom

Withdraw

Withstood

Witness

Witnessed

Won

Wonderful

Worked

Worldwide

Worth

Wow

Write

Wrote

Y

Yes

Yielded

You
Young
Your
Youthful

Z

Zap
Zest
Zestful
Zinger
Zip
Zoom

A

A Child Could Do It

A Cut Above

A Cut Above The Rest

A lot Of

A Must

A Pleasant Experience

A Winner

A Winning Offer

Absolutely No Obligation

Accelerate Your Profits

Accelerate Your Success

Accept My Offer

Accept Our Offer

Act Before It's Too Late

Act Now

Act Today

Added Value

All Free

All Natural

All New

All New Purpose

All The Difference In The World

All You Need

An Exciting Exclusive

An Experience

Anyone Can Do This

Anyone Could Do It

Anyone Could Do This Anywhere Anytime

Approved By Major Companies

As Seen On T.V.

At Your Fingertips

At Your Own Pace

At Your Request

Attractive Offer

Attractive Price

Auto Delivery

Auto Delivery System

Avoid The Crowds

Awesome Bonus Included

Awesome Bonuses

B

Bankruptcy Sale

Bargain Basement Prices Of

Bargain Price

Bargain Price Of

Bargained For

Basement Price

Be First To Qualify

Be The First

Be The First To Qualify

Be Your Own Boss

Beat Factory Direct Prices

Beat The Rush

Beat The System

Beautifully Packaged

Beautifully Positioned

Before And After

Before It's Gone Forever

Before They Are All Gone

Before They Are Gone

Before They're Gone

Behind The Scenes

Behind The Scenes Access

Below Dealer Price

Below Retail Prices

Below Wholesale Prices

Best Buy

Best Performing

Marketing Phrases

Best Quality

Best Selling

Better Quality

Better Than

Big Bonus

Big Bonuses

Big Breakthrough

Big Demand

Bill You Later

Blockbuster Offer

Blown Away

Blown Away The Competition

Blown Out Of The Water

Boggle Your Mind

Bonus Gift

Boost Energy

Boost Sales

Boost Traffic

Both Are Free

Bottom Line

Brand Name

Break The Bank

Bright Future

Brilliant Discovery

Brings Results

Bulk Discount

Bulk Discount Applies
Buy and Get
Buy Direct And Save
Buy Direst
Buy Now
Buy Now And Save
Buy Now And Take Advantage Of
Buy One Get One Free
Buy Today
Buy Today and Save 60%
Buy Two Get One Free
By Popular Demand

C

Call 24 hrs a day
Call Anytime
Call Right Now
Call Today
Call Toll Free
Call Toll Free — Anytime
Cancel Anytime
Captain Of Your Own Ship
Cash Back
Cash Back Guarantee

Marketing Phrases

Cash Discount

Cash Rebate

Change Your Life

Change Your Life Forever

Changes Forever

Check In

Check Out

Christmas Sale

Clear Cut

Clear Value

Clearance Sale

Closeout Sale

Clutter Free

Collector's Item

Commercial Grade Quality

Common Sense Approach

Competitive Advantage

Competitive Edge

Complete Details

Complete Details Inside

Complete Facts

Complete Instructions

Complete Package

Complete Range Of

Complete Setup

Completely Confidential

Power Words For The Sales Professional

Comprehensive Evaluation

Comprehensive Range Of

Comprehensive Support

Comprehensive Training

Computerized Concept

Consumer Help

Consumer Support

Contact Me

Contact Us

Continued Support

Continued Training

Cost Cutting Advantage

Cost Cutting Option

Cost Cutting Packages Available

Cost Cutting Strategies

Cost Cutting Techniques

Cost Effective

Cost Effective Alternative

Cost Effective Option

Crammed With

Credit Cards Accepted

Custom Design

Custom Packages Available

Custom Packaging

Customer Comes First

Customer Satisfaction

Cut Price
Cutting Cost
Cutting Costs
Cutting Edge

D

Dare You
Dealer Price
Dealers Price
Dealt With
Debt Free Options
Decide Now
Deep and Wide
Deep Discount
Delivered To Your Door
Detailed Information
Detailed Training
Details To Follow
Direct To You
Discount Coupons
Discount Equal To Sales Tax
Discover The Difference
Discover Your Freedom

Power Words For The Sales Professional

Discover Your Potential

Doesn't Have To Be

Don't Be Left Behind

Don't Delay

Don't Fall Behind

Don't Miss Out

Don't Miss The Boat

Don't Miss The Opportunity

Don't Miss Your Chance

Don't Miss Your Chance To

Don't Delay

Don't Miss Out

Don't Miss This One

Double Income

Double Your Income

Double Your Money

Double Your Money Back

Double Your Money Back Guarantee

Double Your Paycheck

Double, Triple Your Income

Download Free Trial

Dream Come True

Drive Traffic

Durable And Dynamic

E

Eager Prospects

Earn More

Earn More Money

Earn More Money Now

Earn More Money Today

Ease Of Use

Easy Installation

Easy Operation

Easy Ordering

Easy Payment Options

Easy Payments

Easy To Install

Easy To Read Instructions

Easy To Use

Eliminate Competition

Emerging Growth

Enormous Growth

Enormous Growth Opportunity

Enormous Growth Potential

Enormous Opportunity

Enormous Potential

Envision This

Power Words For The Sales Professional

Error Free
Error Free Reporting
Error Proof
Essential Facts
Essential Ingredient
Everything Provided
Everything Supplied
Everything to Gain
Everything You Need Provided
Everything You Need To Be Successful
Exceed Expectations
Excellent Client Service
Excellent Customer Service
Excellent Offer
Excellent Opportunity
Excellent Opportunity For
Excellent Potential
Excellent Products
Excellent Quality
Excellent Ratings
Excellent Service
Excellent Services
Exciting Details
Exciting Offer
Exclusive Offer
Expect Results

Marketing Phrases

Experience The Difference

Expert Advice

Expert Advice Explained

Expert Opinion

Expert Secrets Reveal

Experts Agree

Experts Approve of

Experts Say

Experts Use

Express Service

Extended Offer

Extensive Research

Extra Benefits

Extra Bonus

Extra Income

Extra Value

Extreme Advertising

Extreme Payoff

Extreme Promotion

Extreme Selling

Extremely Affordable

Extremely Easy

Extremely Informative

Eye Catching

F

Fabulous Facts

Fabulous Offer

Fabulous Opportunity

Fabulous Potential

Fabulous Savings

Fabulous Value

Factory Direct Advantage

Factory Direct Pricing

Factory Direct To You

Fail Proof

Fail Proof System

Fantastic Offer

Fantastic Price

Fast Moving

Fast Results

Fast Service

Fast Setup

Fast Turn Around

Fast Turn Around Time

Faster Service

Featured Product

Features Include

Financing Available

Marketing Phrases

Find The Answer
Find The Answers To
Find The Answers You Have Been Searching For
Fine Quality
Fine Tune
Finest Quality
Finest Quality Available
Fire Sale
Fire The Boss
Fire Your Boss
First Class
First Impression
First Impressions
First Month Free
First Place
Fixed Price
Fixed Rate
Flat Rate
Flexible Options
Flexible Rates
Flexible Terms
Fool Proof Plan
For A Lifetime Of
For A One Time Fee
For A One Time Fee Of
Fraction Of The Cost

Fraction Of The Price

Free Access

Free Advice

Free Approval

Free Booklet

Free Brochure

Free Consultation

Free Coupon

Free Delivery

Free Demo

Free Demonstration

Free Details

Free E-Book

Free Estimate

Free From Pain

Free Get Gift

Free Ideas

Free Issue

Free Membership

Free Newsletter

Free No Obligation

Free Of Charge

Free Offer

Free Replacement

Free Report

Free Sample

Marketing Phrases

Free Special Report
Free Tools
Free Trial Offer
Free Video
Free With Any Purchase
Free With Purchase
Free With Your Order
Free Written Evaluation
Fresh Advice
Fresh Ideas
Fresh Start
Full Access
Full Benefits
Full Color
Full Effect
Full Featured
Full Guarantee
Full Or Part Time
Full Range Of
Full Size
Full Spectrum
Fully Explained
Fully Taught
Fun Program

G

Gaining On

Garage Sale Prices

Get Ahead

Get Ahead In Life

Get In On The Ground Floor

Get Noticed

Get Results

Get Results — Order Now

Get Results Fast

Get Results Overnight

Get Something Extra

Get Something For Yourself

Get Something Good

Get The Best

Get The Facts

Get Your Own Free

Gift With Any Purchase

Gift With Purchase

Go Ahead

Go Ahead You Deserve It

Go At Your Own Pace

Go At Your Pace

Good Judgment

Good Reasons
Good Taste
Good Tasting
Grace Period
Great Opportunity
Ground Floor Offer
Ground Floor Opportunity
Growth Guaranteed
Guaranteed Delivery
Guaranteed Low Price
Guaranteed Lowest Price
Guaranteed Overnight Delivery
Guaranteed Return
Guaranteed To Work
Guaranteed To Work Fast
Guaranteed To Work Quick

H

Hard Hitting
Hard Hitting Facts
Hard Hitting Report
Hassle Free
Have Fun

Power Words For The Sales Professional

Head And Shoulder Above the Rest

Head And Shoulders Above

Heavy Discounts

Heavy Hitter

Heavy Traffic

Helping People Just Like You

Helping People Like You

Here Is The Proof

High Class

High Commission

High Demand

High Growth

High Growth Opportunity

High Impact

High Payout

High Priority

High Rolling

High Speed

High Tech

High Volume

High Volume Discount

Highest Commission Offered

Highest In Its Class

Highest Paid

Highest Rated

Highlighted In

Highly Rated
Highly Recommended
Holiday Extravaganza
Holiday Price
Holiday Sale
Holiday Special
Holiday Special Sale
Honor And Hope
Hot Item
Hot Property
Hot Sale
Hottest Opportunity
Hottest Price
Huge Demand
Huge Difference
Huge Discounts
Hurry Offer Ends Soon

I

Idiot Proof
If You Decide
Immediate Impact
Immediate Response
Immediate Response Important

Power Words For The Sales Professional

Immediate Response Necessary

Immediate Response Required

Important Facts

Improve Your Financial Position

Improve Your Life

Improve Your Relationships

Improved Version

In A Flash

In Demand

In Demand Solutions

In Depth

In Minutes

In Need

In Seconds

In Store Repairs

In Stores Now

Incentive For Buying

Incentive For Purchasing Today

Increase Earning Power

Increase Knowledge

Increase Your Earning Power

Increase Your Payout

Increase Your Profit

Increase Your Profit Immediately

Increasing Amount

Increasingly

Marketing Phrases

Increasingly In Demand

Incredible Benefits

Incredible Response Guaranteed

Incredibly Easy To Use

Incredibly Insightful

Inexpensive Incredible Option

Inflation-Beating

Informative In Minutes

Insane Bonuses

Insane Offer

Insane Price Reductions

Insane Prices

Insane Special Offer

Insane Value

Insider Benefits

Insider Information

Inspired Action

Instant Access

Instant Success

Instructive Report Shows You How To

Intelligent Decision

Interest Free

Interest Free Financing

Interesting Report Reveals

Intriguing Report Reveals

Intriguing Results

Power Words For The Sales Professional

Introducing Introductory Offer
Introductory Offer
Introductory Rate
Ironclad Guarantee
Is Provided With
It Makes Sense Buy Now
It Sells
It Sells Its Self
It Will Boggle Your Mind
It's A Breeze
It's A Must
It's A No Brainer
It's An Incredible Value
It's Confidential
It's Easy
It's Here
It's Just That Easy
It's That Easy
It's All Here
It's Final Here
It's Free
It's Your Choice

J

Join The Winners
Join The Winners Circle
Just Arrived
Just Because You Can
Just Do It
Just In Time
Just In Time For The Holidays
Just In Time For The Summer

K

Keeping Up With The Times
Keeping You Number One
Keeping You Number One Is Our Priority
Killer Application
Killer Investment Opportunity
Killer Prices
Killer Strategies To Take You Further
Killer Strategy
Killer Tactics
Killer Techniques That Will Show You How To
Kind Considerate And Caring

Kindly Taking You Further
King Size Bargain
King Size Deal
Know How
Knowledgeable Expert Reveals

L

Large Bargains
Large Savings
Large Selection
Larger Than Life
Largest Of Its Kind
Largest Selection
Largest Selling
Last Chance
Last Chance Join Now
Last Chance To Buy
Last Chance To Own
Last Minute
Last Minute Deal
Last Minute Savings
Lasting Impression
Lasting Savings
Lasting Value

Marketing Phrases

Late Breaking
Latest Craze
Latest Technology
Leading Experts Agree
Leading Name
Leading Name Brand
Leading Strategies
Leading Tactics
Leading Techniques
Leading Technology
Learn About
Learn At Your Own Pace
Learn Something New
Learn The Secrets
Learn The Secrets To
Lease To Buy
Leasing Is Available
Legendary Savings
Less Hassle
Lifetime Guarantee
Lifetime Income
Lifetime Warranty
Light Weight
Like No Other
Limited Time
Limited Time Offer

Limited Time Offer Don't Delay
Limited Time Offer Don't Wait
Limited Time Offer Hurry
Limited-Time Offer — May Be Withdrawn At Any Time
Little Known Secrets
Live Your Dream
Long Lasting
Long Term
Low Factory Prices
Low Interest
Low Price
Low Price Of
Low Risk Solution
Lower Prices
Lowest Price Ever
Low-Risk Solution
Loyalty Program
Loyalty Sale
Luxury Living

M

Magical Savings
Mail Today
Mainstream Solution

Marketing Phrases

Maintained By

Major Sale

Make $1,000 Per Week

Make A Choice

Make Money

Make Money Now

Make The Right Choice

Makes A Great Gift

Makes Sense

Mammoth Mania

Mammoth Sale

Marked Down

Massive Amount

Massive Offer

Massive Sale

Massive Savings

Master Of Your Destiny

Master Your Destiny

Master Your Doubts

Master Your Fear

Master Your Finances

Master Your Future

Master Your Income

Master Your Problems

Master Yourself

Measure Up

Power Words For The Sales Professional

Mega Millions

Mega Promotion

Mega Sale

Mega Savings

Mega Savings Event

Millions Of People

Millions Of People Just Like You Already Have

Millions Of People Like You

Millions Sold

Mind-Blowing

Minimal Invest

Minimal Investment

Minimal Investment Maximum Return

Minimal Investment Required

Minimal Investment Today

Minimum Effort

Minimum Effort Involved

Minimum Effort Required

Minimum Investment

Minimum Work

Minimum Work With Maximum Results

Modeled After The Highly Successful

Modern Miracle

Money Making

Money Making Facts

Money Making Secrets

Marketing Phrases

Money Making Secrets Revealed

Money Making Strategies

Money Making Strategies Revealed

Money Making System

Money Making Techniques

Money Making Techniques Revealed

Money Making Tips

Money Making Tips Revealed

Money Off

Money Saving

Money Saving Deal

Money Saving Program

Monumental Decision

Monumental Sale

Most Comprehensive

Most Requested

Most Underrated

Mouth Watering

Multi-Functional

Multifunctional Program

Multiple Bonuses

Multiple Gifts

Multiple Income Sources

Multiple Income Streams

Multiple Revenue Sources

Multiple Revenue Streams

Multiple Streams Of Income

Must Have

N

National Best Seller

National Brand

Nationally Known

Nationally Recognized

Natural Growth

Necessary Skills

New And Improved

New And Used

New Frontier

New Niche

New Vision

New Way

Next Day Air Available

Next Frontier

Next-Day Air Available

No Additional Fees

No Application Fee

No Catch

No Commitments

No Doubt

Marketing Phrases

No Experience Necessary
No Experience Needed
No Fees
No Hassle
No Hassle Guarantee
No Hassle Refund
No Hassles
No Hype
No Interest For One Year
No Minimum Order
No Money Down
No Money Required
No Nonsense
No Obligation
No One Will Call
No One Will Call You
No Out Of Pocket Expense
No Out-Of-Pocket Cash
No Payment For (X) Months
No Payment For One Year
No Payment For
No Payments For 6 Months
No Postage Necessary
No Problem
No Questions Asked
No Questions Asked Guarantee

Power Words For The Sales Professional

No Questions Asked Refund

No Restriction

No Restrictions Apply

No Risk

No Sales Person Will Call

No Salesperson Will Visit

No Upfront Money Required

No-Hassles Refund

No-Nonsense

Not Available Anywhere Else

Not Available In Stores

Not In Stores

Nothing Better

Nothing Else Required

Nothing Else To Buy

Nothing Else To Buy- Ever

Nothing To Lose

Novel Ideas

Now Available

Now Available For A Limited Time

Now Is The Time

Now Is the Time To Take Control Of Your

Now Is Your Chance

Now More Powerful

Number-One

O

Oder While Supplies Last

Of The Year

Offer Ends (Date)

Offer Ends Soon

Offer Ends

Offer Limited To First 20 Customers

Offer Limited To First(X) Orders

Once In A Lifetime

Once In A Lifetime Chance

Once In A Lifetime Chance To Own

Once In A Lifetime Offer

Once In A Lifetime Opportunity

One Hour Service

One Time Setup Fee

Only $9.99

Open (X) Days A Week

Open (X) Hours A Day

Option To Choose

Option To Purchase

Order Direct

Order Now

Order Today

Order While Supplies Last

Original Offer
Others Cost Twice As Much
Outdated Strategies
Outdated Techniques
Out-Of-Sight
Outstanding Benefits
Outstanding Purchase
Overnight Delivery
Overwhelming Odds
Overwhelming Response
Own It Outright

P

Participation Is Limited
Participation Limited
Patent Pending Program
Patented Technology
Pay Later
Pay Only $9.95
Pays Off
People Helping People
Perfect Performance
Perfect Performance Every Time
Performance Guaranteed

Marketing Phrases

Permanent Income

Permanent Protection

Personal Fortune

Personal Guarantee

Personal Perspective

Personalized Options

Personalized Program

Phenomenal Offer

Phenomenal Opportunity

Phenomenal Personal Growth

Phenomenal Program

Phone Today

Pick Up The Phone Today

Pioneered Technology

Pioneered The Program

Pioneers In

Plus Get

Plus Receive

Powerful And Practice

Powerful Program

Practical Guide

Precision Programming

Premier Event

Preview Before You Buy

Preview Before You Purchase

Price Comparison

Price Comparison Program

Price Cut

Price Includes Shipping

Priced Below Competitors Price

Priced Below Market value

Prices Below Competitors

Prices Cut In Half

Prices Slashed

Prime Quality

Private Invitation

Private Invitation Sale Only

Professional Product

Profit Generating

Profit Generating System

Proven Record

Proven Track Record

Purchasing Power

Q

Qualified Buyers Only

Qualified Quality

Quality Guaranteed

Quality Minded

Quality Pricing

Quality Products
Quantity Pricing
Queen of
Question: (INSERT THE QUESTION)
Quick Special
Quick Tips

R

Rank High
Ranked At The Top
Ranked At The Top Of The Class
Ranked Highest In Its Class
Rapid Change
Rare Chance
Rare Interview Reveals
Rare Opportunity
Rare Opportunity To Own
Rare Rate Reduction
Rare Rates
Rates As Low As
Rave Reviews
Read All About It
Ready To Use
Ready To Win

Power Words For The Sales Professional

Real People
Real Testimonials
Realize Your Dream
Reap The Benefits
Reap The Rewards
Receive (INSERT PROMOTIONAL) Free
Receive Additional Bonuses
Receive Coupon With Payment
Receive Free With
Recognized As
Recommended By
Recruited By
Red Hot
Red Hot Info
Red Hot Opportunity
Red Hot Product
Red Hot Reductions
Red Hot Sale
Reduced Costs
Reduced Payments
Reduced Price
Reduced Rates
Register For Your Free
Register Here
Register Today
Remarkable Breakthrough Product

Marketing Phrases

Remarkable Results

Rent To Own

Respected Name

Results Focused

Results Guaranteed

Results In Days

Results In Minutes

Results In Weeks

Results Minded

Results Orientated

Results Overnight

Return It And own Nothing

Return On Investment

Revealing Report

Revised and Updated

Revised Conditions

Revised Edition

Revised Report

Revolutionary Money Making Program

Revolutionary Product

Revolutionary Report Reveals

Revolutionary Secrets

Revolutionary Strategy

Rewarded Richly

Right Now

Right To Be Free From

Right To Be Happy
Risk Free
Risk Free Offer
Risk Free Trial
Risk Nothing
Risk-Free Trial
Riveting Report
Riveting Sales
Roaring Reviews
Rock Bottom Price
Rock Bottom Prices
Run With The Big Dogs
Runs Like New
Rush Delivery
Rush Delivery Available

S

Safe And Secure
Safe For The Environment
Safe To The Environment
Safer Than
Sale Ends Tomorrow
Same As Cash
Same Day Delivery

Marketing Phrases

Same Day Service

Satisfaction Guarantee

Save Effort

Save Hundreds

Save Money

Save Thousands

Save Time

Save Your Sanity

Saver Sale

Savvy Savers

Savvy Savers Sale

Secret Site

Secrets Revealed

Secrets Revealed In This

Secure Savings

Secure Your Future

Secure Your Opportunity

Secure Your Time Today

Secure Yours Today

Secured Opportunity

See Before You Buy

See For Yourself Before You Buy

See The Difference

See The Savings

Send For Free Details

Send For Your Free Report

Power Words For The Sales Professional

Send Now

Send Today

Send Your Name

Sensational Price

Sensational Product

Sensational Savings

Sensational Service

Sensational Site

Sense Of Security

Sensible Safe And Secure

Service Minded

Set Your Own Hours

Setting High Standards

Shape Your Body

Shape Your Life

Shape Your Own Future

Shape Your Own Tomorrow

Shape Your Tomorrow

Short-Term Lease

Sign Up For Free Today

Significant Savings

Significantly Improve

Simple Solutions

Simple Step

Simple Steps

Simple To Start

Marketing Phrases

Simple To Use

Simplified Process

Simply Irresistible

Simply Powerful

Simply The Best

Sky-Rocketed Sales

Slashing Prices

Small Investment

Smart Buy

Smart Investment

Smart Move

Smart Strategies

Smarter Way

Snowball Effect

Soar Above

Special Bonus

Special Discounts

Special Offer

Special Price

Special Report

Special Rewards Program

Special Savings Program

Special Service Program

Special Training Available

Specializing In

Speed Delivery

Power Words For The Sales Professional

Stable Company
Stand Out
Stand Out From The Crowd
Start Earning
Start Earning The Income You Deserve
Start Living Your Life
Start Making Money Now
Start Making Money Today
Start Saving Today
Start With Nothing Down
Startling Facts
Startling Results
Start-Up
State Of The Art Facility
State Of The Art Program
State Of The Art Technology
State-Of-The-Art
Stay Ahead Of The Competition
Stay Competitive
Step By Step Development
Step By Step Instruction
Step By Step Training Program
Step-By-Step
Step-By-Step Guide
Step-By-Step Instructions
Stop Running Away From The Reality

Marketing Phrases

Stop Spinning Your Wheels

Stop Wasting Money

Stop Wasting Time

Stop Wasting Time

Stop Wasting Your Effort

Stop Wasting Your Hard Earned Money

Stop Wasting Your Life

Stop Wasting Your Talent

Stop Wasting Your Time

Strong Reputation

Strong Sturdy And Safe

Substantial Savings

Substantiated Savings

Super Deal

Super Sale

Super Saver

Super Site

Superior Living

Superior Product

Superior Savings

Superior Staff

Sure Bet

Sure Fire

Sure Fire Way To Get Ahead

Sure Fire Way To Results

Sure Fire Way To Save

Sure To Fit Your Budget
Sure To Fit Your Lifestyle
Sure To Make Your Neighbors Jealous
Sure To Make Your Wife
Surging Past The Competition
Surprise Bonus
Surprise Bonus Included
Surprise Guest

T

Take Action
Take Action Now
Take Action Today
Take Action While You Still Can
Take Advantage
Take Advantage Of
Take Care Of
Take Charge Of
Take Control
Take Over
Taking Over
Taking Over The Market
Tax Benefits
Tax Deductible

Marketing Phrases

Terrific Price
Test Drive
Test Drive Today
Test it For Yourself
Test It Free
Test Prove There Is Nothing Like It
Tested And Approved
Tests Prove
The Best
The Truth About
There's Nothing Else Like It
This Is Your Chance
Thousand Sold
Thousands Agree
Thousands Can't Be Wrong
Thousands Of Happy Customers
Thousands Saved
Thousands Sold
Time Is Running Out
Time Saving
Time Sensitive
Time Tested
Time Tested Tip Reveals
Time-Limited Information
Times Running Out
Time-Saving

Power Words For The Sales Professional

Time-Tested
Tip Of The Day
Tip Of The Iceberg
To Your Benefit
To Your Future
Today's Special
Today's Tip
Toll Free Call
Top Business
Top Level
Top Name
Top Of The Line
Top Producers Love
Top Producers Tip
Top Secret
Top Secret Formula
Total Makeover
Total Remake
Total System
Travel Discounts
Tremendous Benefit
Tremendous Growth Potential
Tremendous Opportunity
Tremendous Response
Tremendous Savings
Tried And True

Triple Your Money Back
Trouble Free
True Facts
True Skills
True Techniques
Truly An Incredible Opportunity
Truly Unbelievable
Trusted Company
Try Before You Buy
Try It Now
Tue Good To Be True
Two Free Bonuses

U

Ultimate Blowout Special
Ultimate In
Ultimate In Savings
Ultimate Super Sale
Ultimate System For
Unbeatable Savings
Unbeatable Strategies
Unbelievable Bargain
Unbelievable Bargains
Unbelievable Opportunity

Power Words For The Sales Professional

Unbelievable Price

Unconditional Guarantee

Uncovered Secrets

Under Priced

Under Priced By Hundreds

Unique Benefits

Unique Offer

Unique Opportunity

Unique Plan

Unique Strategies

Unique System

Universal System

Universal Truths

Unlike Any Other

Unlimited Growth

Unlimited Growth Opportunity

Unlimited Income

Unlimited Opportunity

Unlimited Potential

Unlimited Sales

Unlimited Support

Unlimited Time

Unlimited Warranty

Unlock The Secrets

Unlock Your Hidden Potential

Unlock Your Potential

Marketing Phrases

Unlock Your Success
Unlock Your Talents
Unlock Yourself From
Unparalleled In The Market
Unsurpassed In Client Service
Unsurpassed In The Market
Untapped Clients
Untapped Customers
Untapped Industry
Untapped Market
Untapped Potential
Untapped Revenue
Untapped Sales
Untapped Stream Of Income
Untold Until Now
Updated Edition
Updated Report
Upgrade For Free
Upgrade For Only
Upgrade Now
Up-Scale
Urgent Matter
Use Your Credit Card
Useful Benefits

V

Valuable Information

Valuable Vision

Value And Savings Combined

Value And Variety

Value For Your Dollar

Value Packed

Value Packed Offer

Value-Added

Variety Pack

Versatile Product

Very Hot

Very Hot Opportunity

Vibrant And Full

Vital Information

Vital Piece Of Information

Vital Purchase

Vital To Your Business

Vital To Your Future

Vital To Your Happiness

Vital To Your Success

W

We Did It And So Can You

We Need Your Help

We Pay Postage And Handling

We Pay Shipping And Handling

We Really Care

We Take A Common Sense Approach

We Value Your Opinion

We Want To Know

We Will Deliver

We Will Not Sell Your Name

Wealth Building

Wealth Clients

Wealth Secrets Revealed

Wealthy Expert Reveals

Weird Story You Must Read

While Supplies Last

While We Still Can

Wholesale Prices

Why Not

Why Wait

Wide Range Of

Wide Range Of Options

Wide Range Of Supplies

Wide Variety
Wider Variety
Will To Win
Will You Be The One
With This You Wont Need To
Without Lifting A Finger
Word Of Mouth
Works In Minutes
Works While You Sleep
World Premier
World's Greatest
World's Largest
Worth Its Weight In Gold
Worth The Wait

Y

Year-Round
You Are Valuable To Us
You Be The Boss
You Can Do It
You Can Do It And We Can Help
You Can Do This
You Can Too
You Can Win With This

You Choose
You Deserve
You Our Clients Come First
You Owe It To Yourself
You Qualify
You Select
You Should
You The Customer Comes First
You're The Boss
Your Benefit
Your Choice
Your Choice Of
Your Choice Of Selection
Your Future

Z

Zero Confusion
Zero Down
Zero Hassle
Zero Headaches
Zero In
Zero To One Hundred
Zip In To Get Your Free
Zoom In On The Big Picture

Miscellaneous

#1 Product/Service/Business

% Money-Back Guarantee

% Off

(X) Made Me (Y)

(X) Easy Payments

(X) Years' Experience

1 Simple Step

100%

100% Beneficial

100% Fail Proof

100% Money Back Guarantee

100% Proof

100% Satisfaction

30 Day Money Back Guarantee

30 Days Free

A

5 Days Only
Act Now
Act Quickly
Add To Cart
Add To Your
Apply Today
Available For Immediate Download
Available Immediately

B

Be Sure To
Best Value
Book And Save
Book It Now
Book Now
Buy And Save
Buy Now
Buy Today

C

Call Now
Call Today
Call Us This Week To Schedule An Appointment
Certified Expert
Check Our
Check Out
Check This Out
Choose Your
Click Button
Click For More
Click Here
Click Here To Find Out All The Details
Click Here To Get Started Today
Click Here To Watch The Video
Come See Our Prices
Compare Prices
Contact Now
Contact Us
Contact Us Today

D

Discover Your
Do Not Buy Unless

Don't Be Left Out
Don't Forget To
Don't Miss
Don't Wait
Don't Wait Another Second
Donate Today
Download Now

E

Easy To
Enroll Now
Expires At Midnight Tonight.
Expires In

F

Find Items
Find Out More
Find Savings
Find Yours
Follow This
For A Short Time Only
For Even Faster Service, Call
For More Details Call
Free Action Guide

Free Consultation
Free Guide
Free Shipping

G

Get A Free Quote Today
Get A Free Trial
Get A Quote
Get Access Today
Get Free
Get It Here
Get It Now
Get More Info Here
Get The Best
Get Your
Get Your Copy Today
Get Your Free Copy Today
Get Yours Now
Get Yours Today
Give A Gift

H

How To
Hurry

I

I Can't Wait To Hear From You

I Encourage You To

I Invite You To

I Urge You To Act At Once

I Urge You To Send for Your Free Brochure

Immediate Download

In A Hurry? Call

Instant Download

Investigate

It's Important That You Respond Promptly

J

Join Now

Join Today

Join Us

Just Hit Reply And We'll Email You The Details

Just Reach For Your Phone

L

Learn More

Learn More About Us At *yourwebsite.com*

Learn To
Limited Availability
Limited Time Offer
Limited Time Only
Look At

M

Mail This Convenient Coupon Today
Mail Your Order Today
Money Back
Money Back Guarantee

N

Need More
No Experience Necessary
No Fees
No Obligation
No Questions Asked Guarantee
Now You Can

O

Offer Expires
Offer Expires September 1st

Order Now
Order Now And Receive A Free Gift
Order Now, While There's Still Time
Order Your

P

Pay Less
Place Your Order Now, While Everything Is Still In Front Of You.
Please Don't Hesitate To Call Us
Please See
Please View Our
Purchase

R

Read Reviews
Register
Register Now
Reply Today
Request For Free Quote
Request Your FREE Quote Today
Request Yours Today
Research
Reserve

Call To Action

Reserve Now
Reserve Your Spot Now
Respond By
Rush Today

S

Satisfaction Guaranteed
Save Big
Save Money
Save Now
Save On
Save Today
Save Up To
Save With
Search For
Search Now
Search Our
See Deals
See It In Action
See More
See Our Coupon
See Our Products
See Pricing
Send For
Send For Our Free Catalog

Send In Your Application Today

Shop At

Shop Low Prices

Shop Now

Shop Online

Shop Today

Show Price

Sign Me Up Now

Sign Up

Sign Up For Your Free Trial Immediately

Sign Up Here

Sign Up now

Sign Up Now While You Still Can

Sign Up Online At *yourwebsite.com*

Sign Up Today

Start Now

Start Today

Start Your Free Trial Now

Stock Up

Submit Now

T

Take A Closer Look

Take A Look At

Take Action Now

Take Action Today
Take The Tour
Talk To An Expert
The Most Important Call You Will Make Today
To Place Your Order, Call Us Tool Free At
Tour Our
Try It Free
Try It Today
Try Us Out Now

V

View All Products
View Features
Visit our
Visit Us At

W

Watch For
Watch Our Tutorial
We'd Like To Hear From You
We're Waiting For Your Call
Why Not Give Us A Call To Find Out All The Details
Why Wait

Y

Yes, I Want To Get Started Today
You Might Also Try
You Might Consider
Your Free Trial Is Just A Click Away
Yours For Asking

About the Author

Justin lives in middle Tennessee with his wife and three children. He is recognized as an expert in sales, leadership and personal development. His success has put him on a virtual platform with the leading experts such as Anthony Robbins, Brain Tracy, and Zig Ziglar.

Justin's diverse professional career in politics, law enforcement, and business allows him to bring fresh perspectives to the discussion. His unique ability to connect with an audience has made him a sought after speaker. His workshops and seminars on Sales, Leadership, and Personal Development, are inspiring a new generation to reach past their potential.

Connect with him at,

www.JustinHammonds.com

For FREE
Sales & Leadership Videos
Go To

www.JustinHammonds.com